Baking Cakes

Story by Neil Griffiths

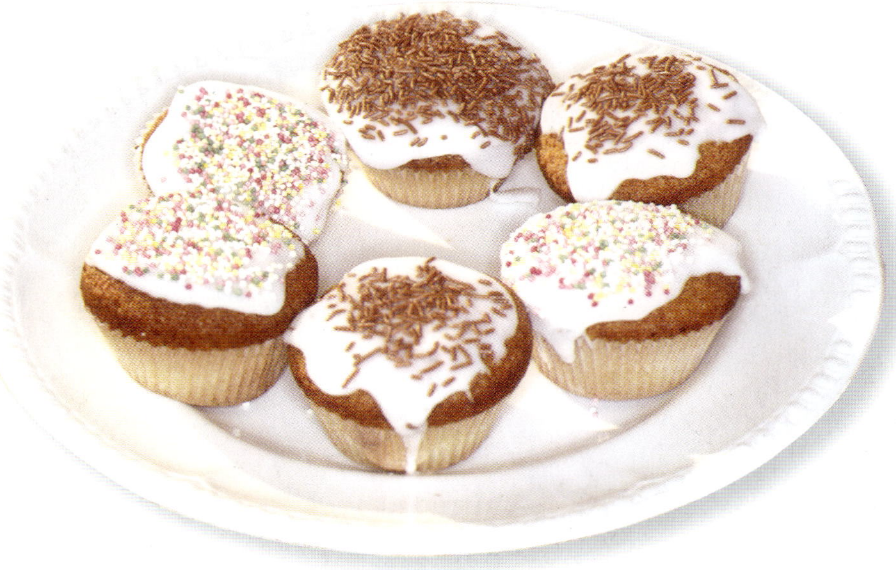

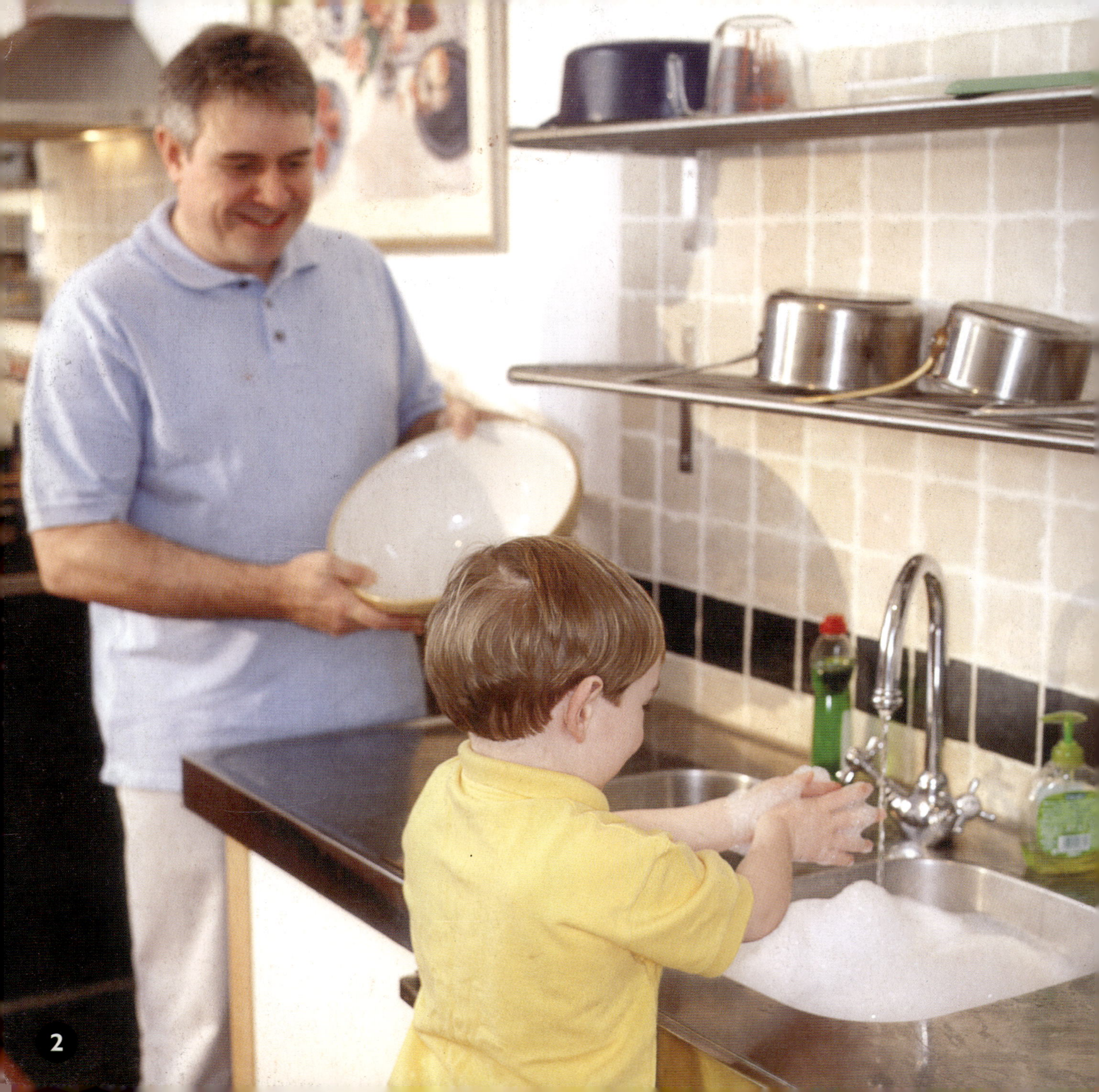

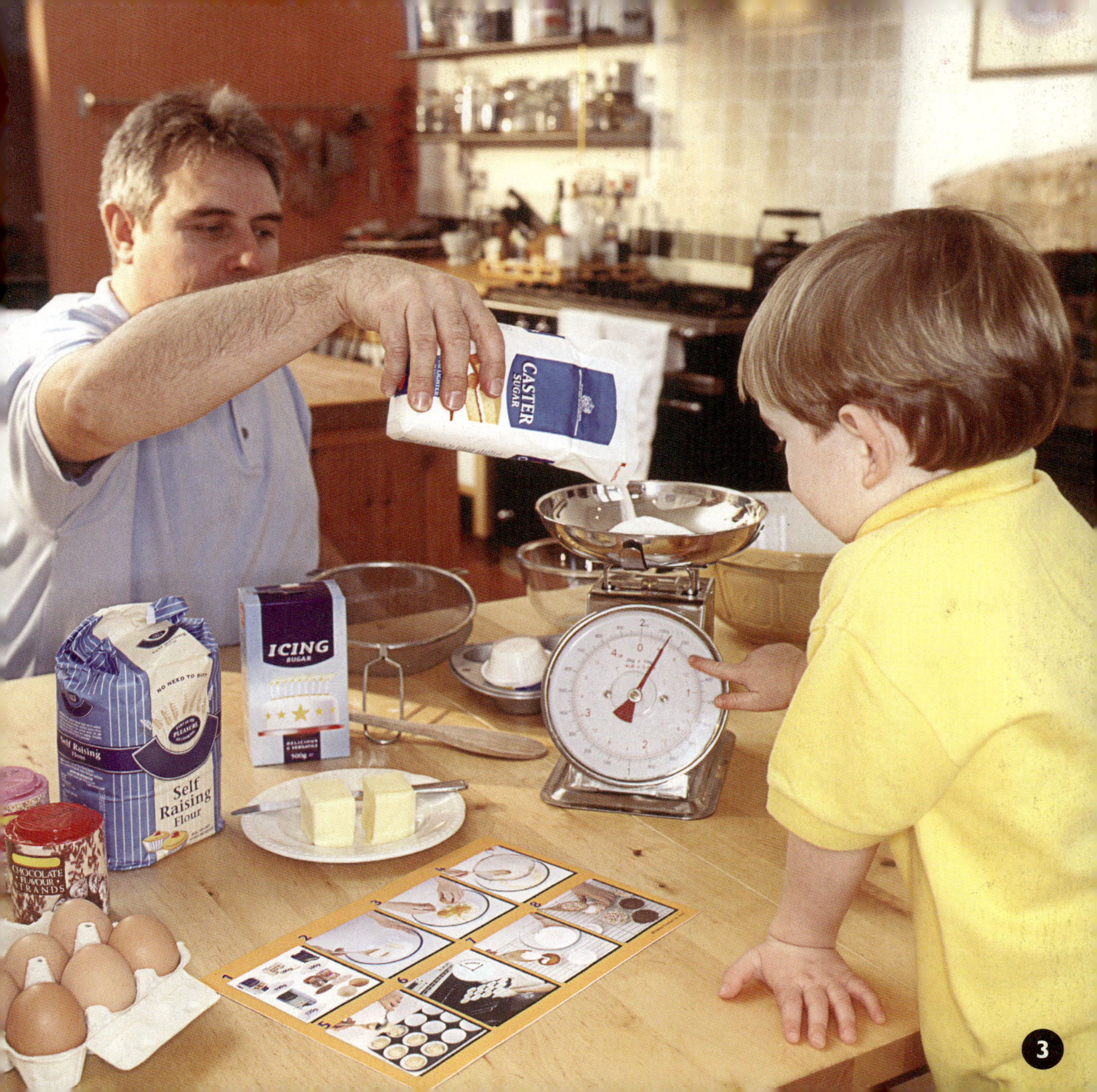
CASTER
SUGAR
ICING
SUGAR
Self Raising Flour
Self
Raising
Flour
CHOCOLATE
FLAVOUR
STRANDS

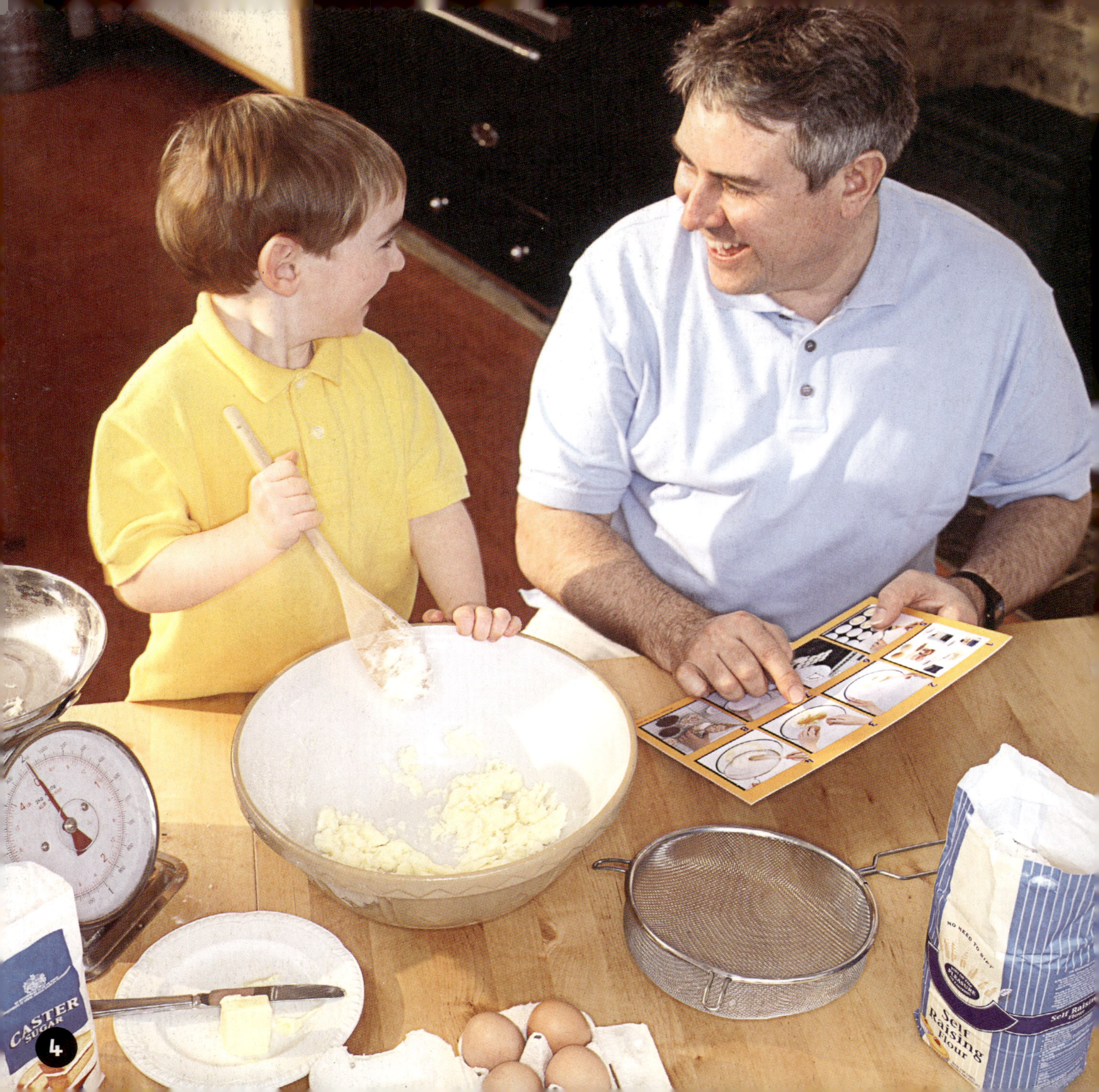
CASTER SUGAR
Self Raising Flour

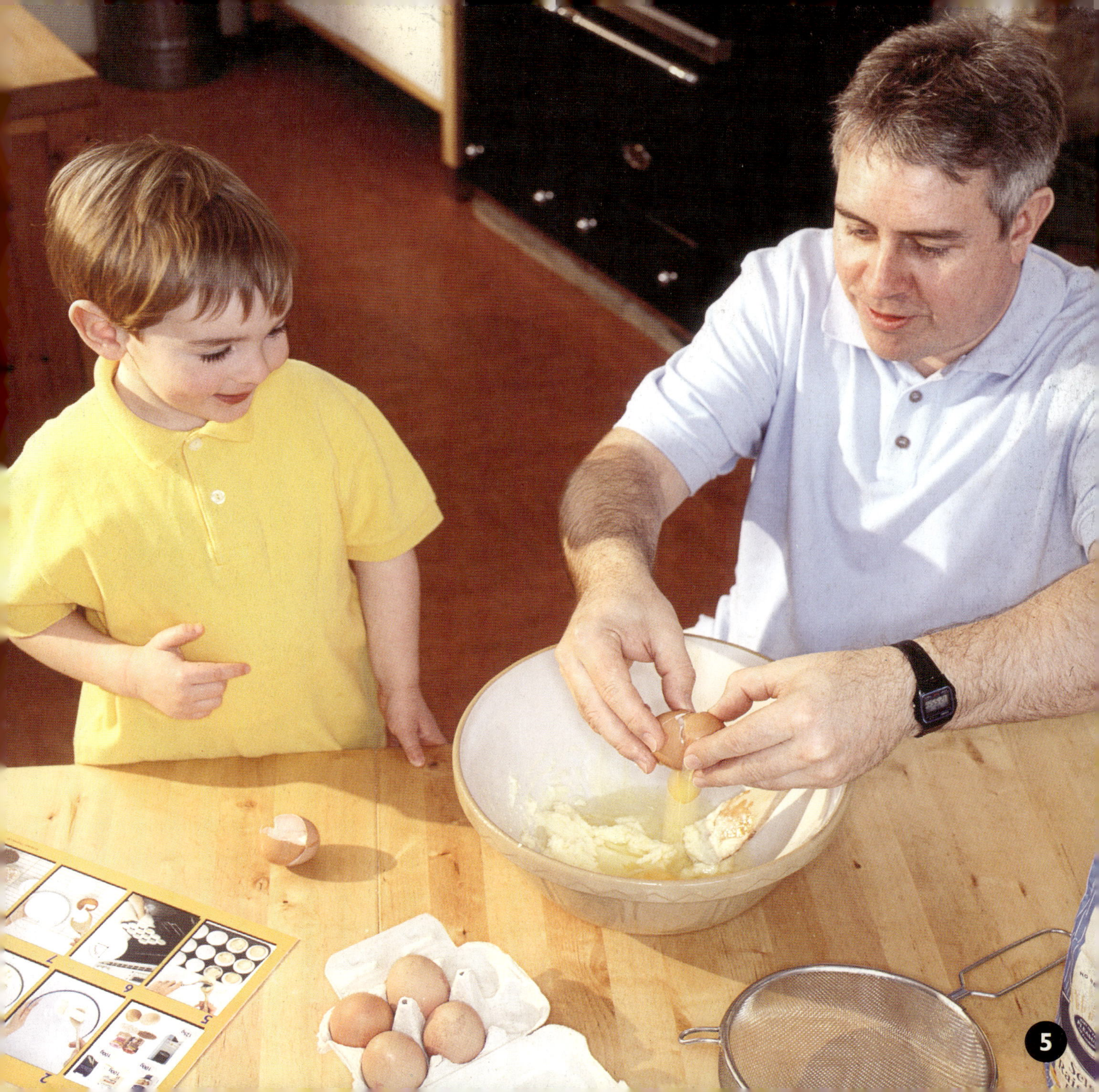

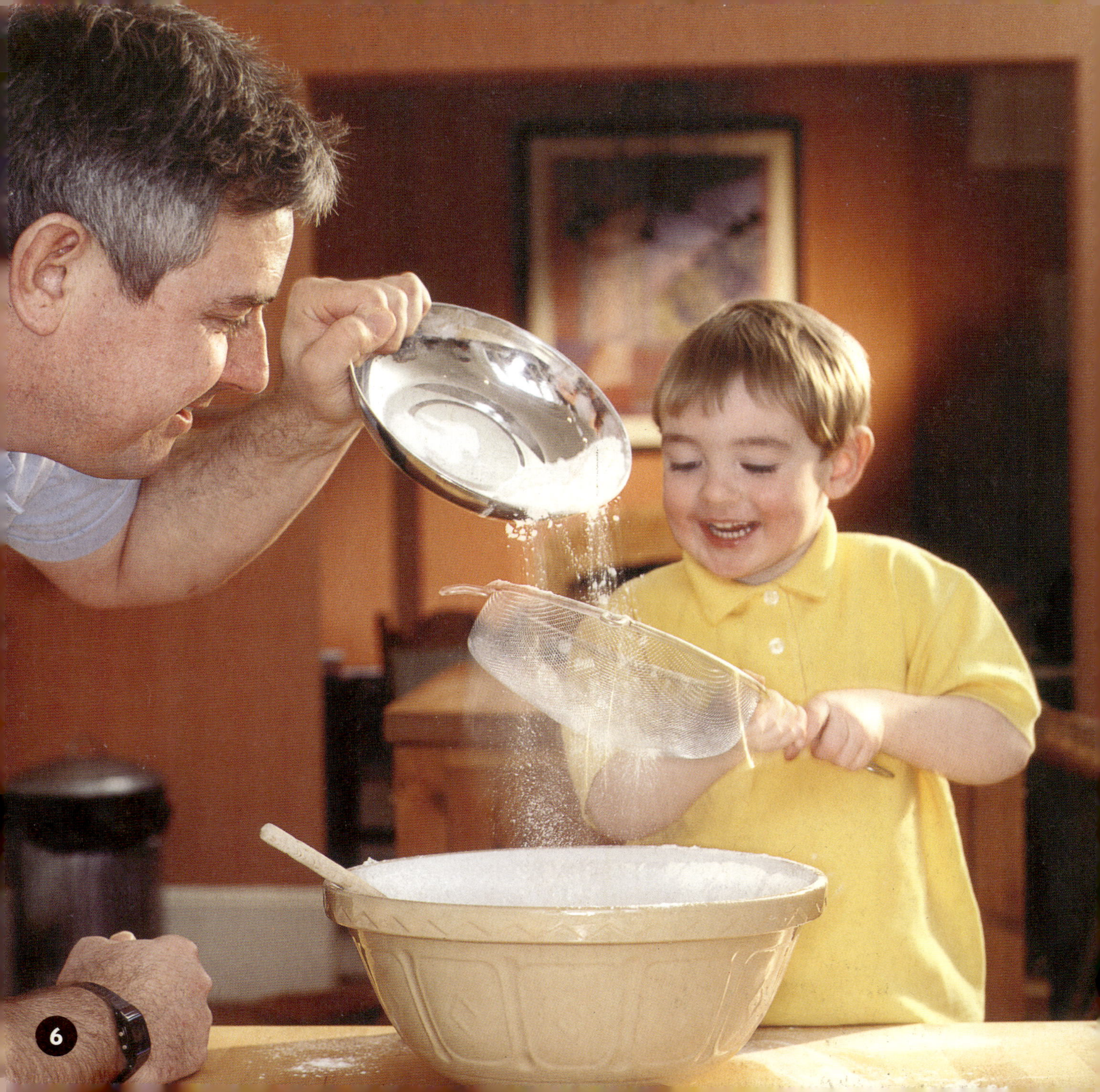

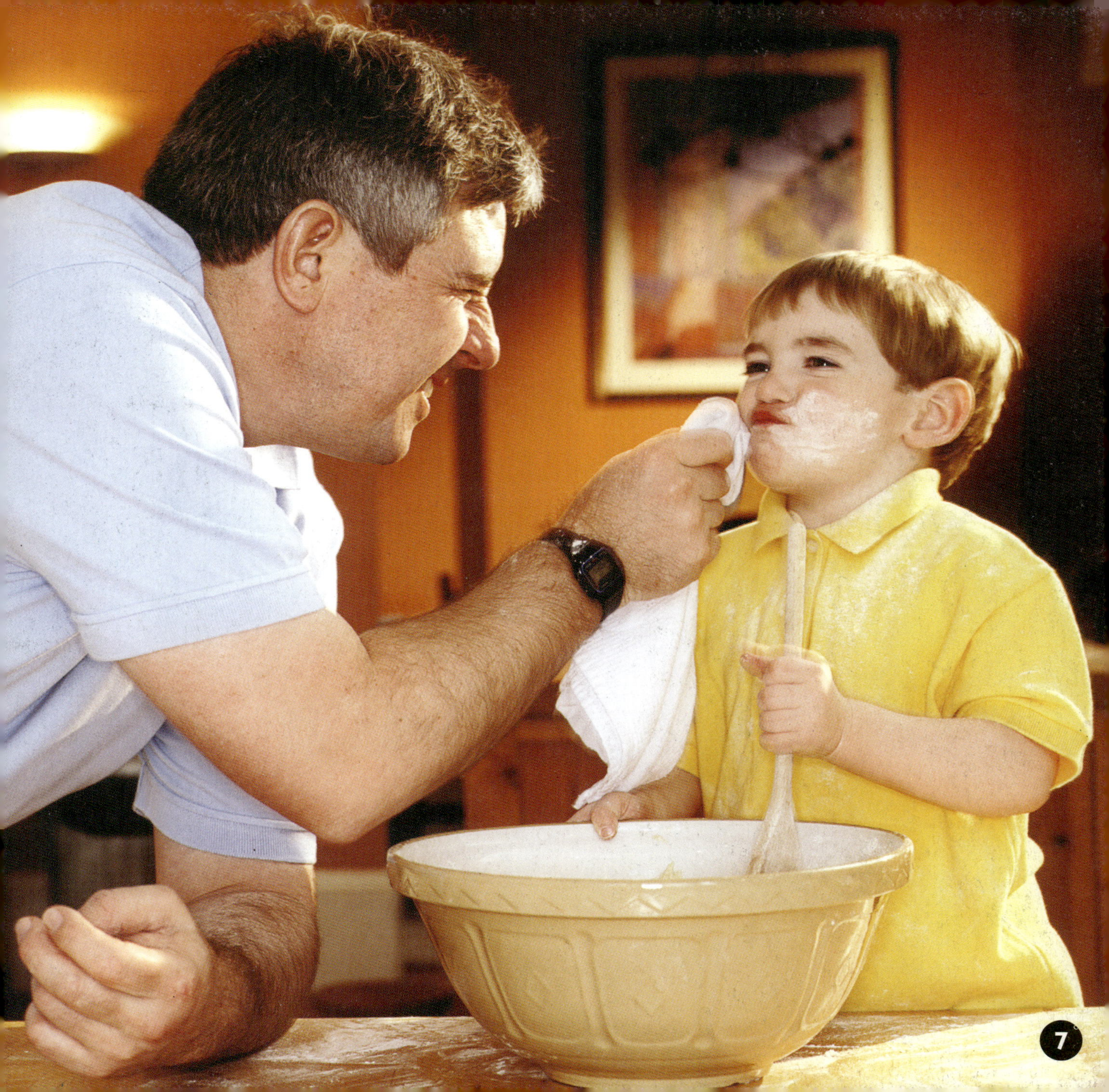

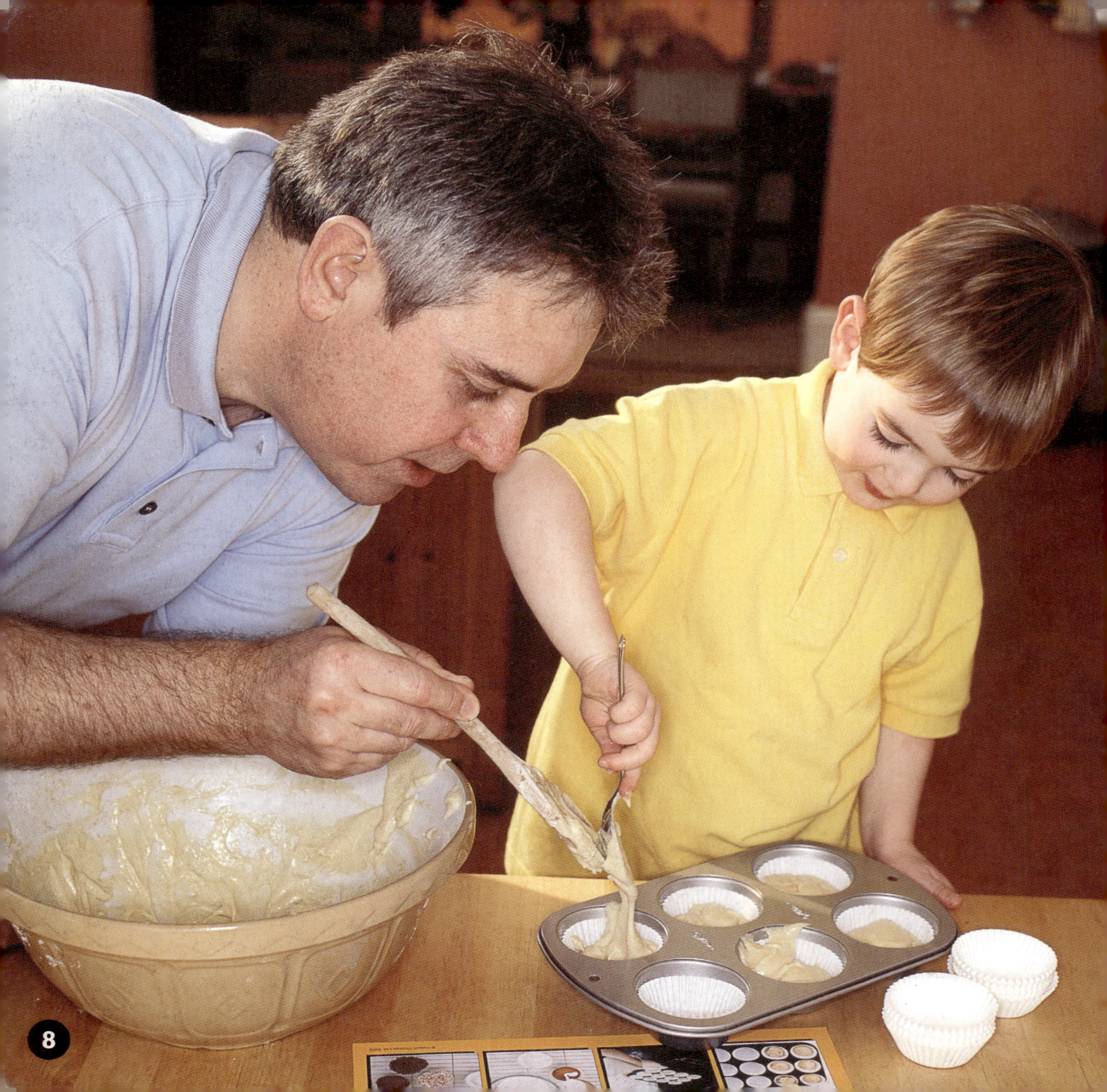

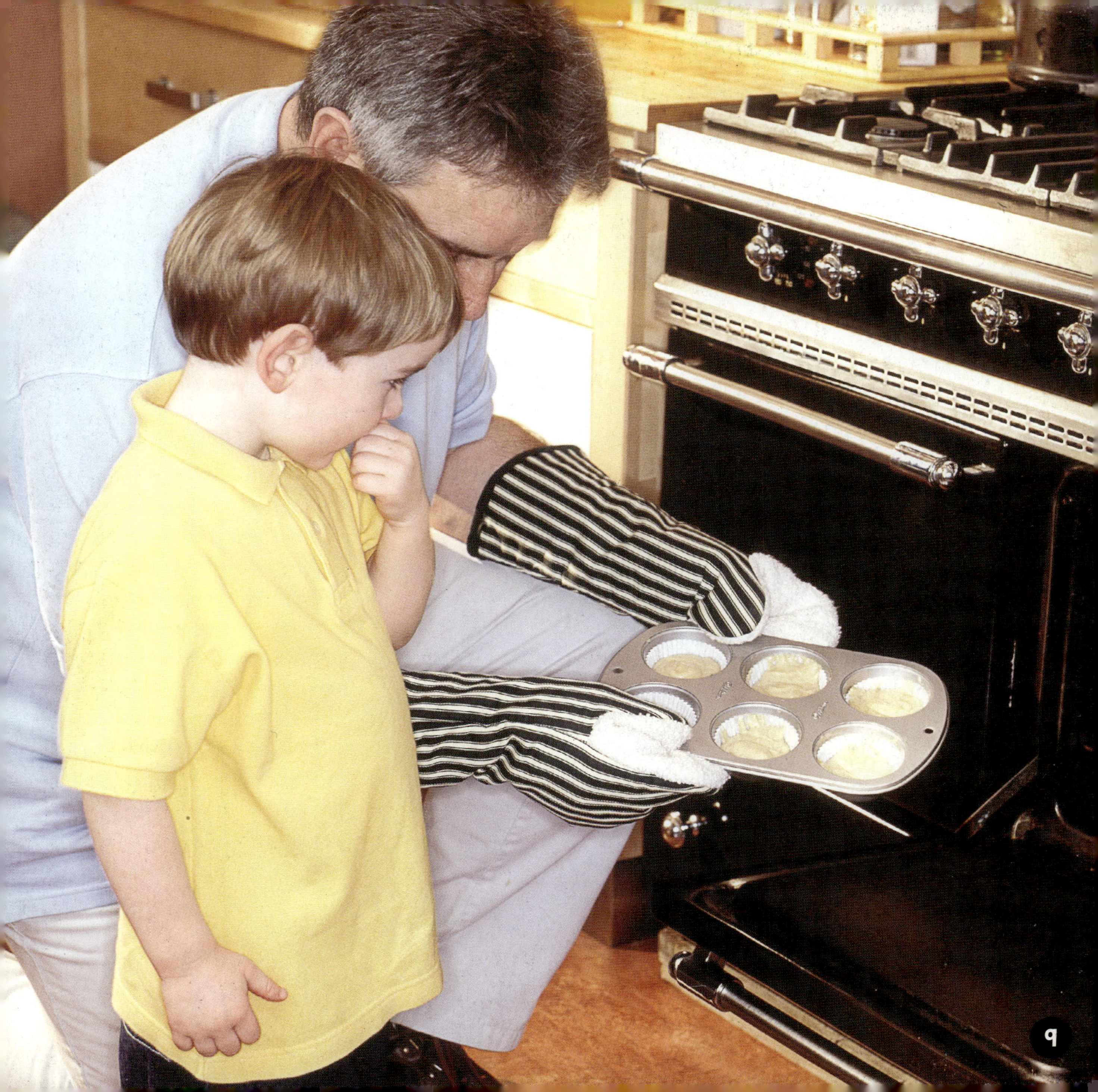

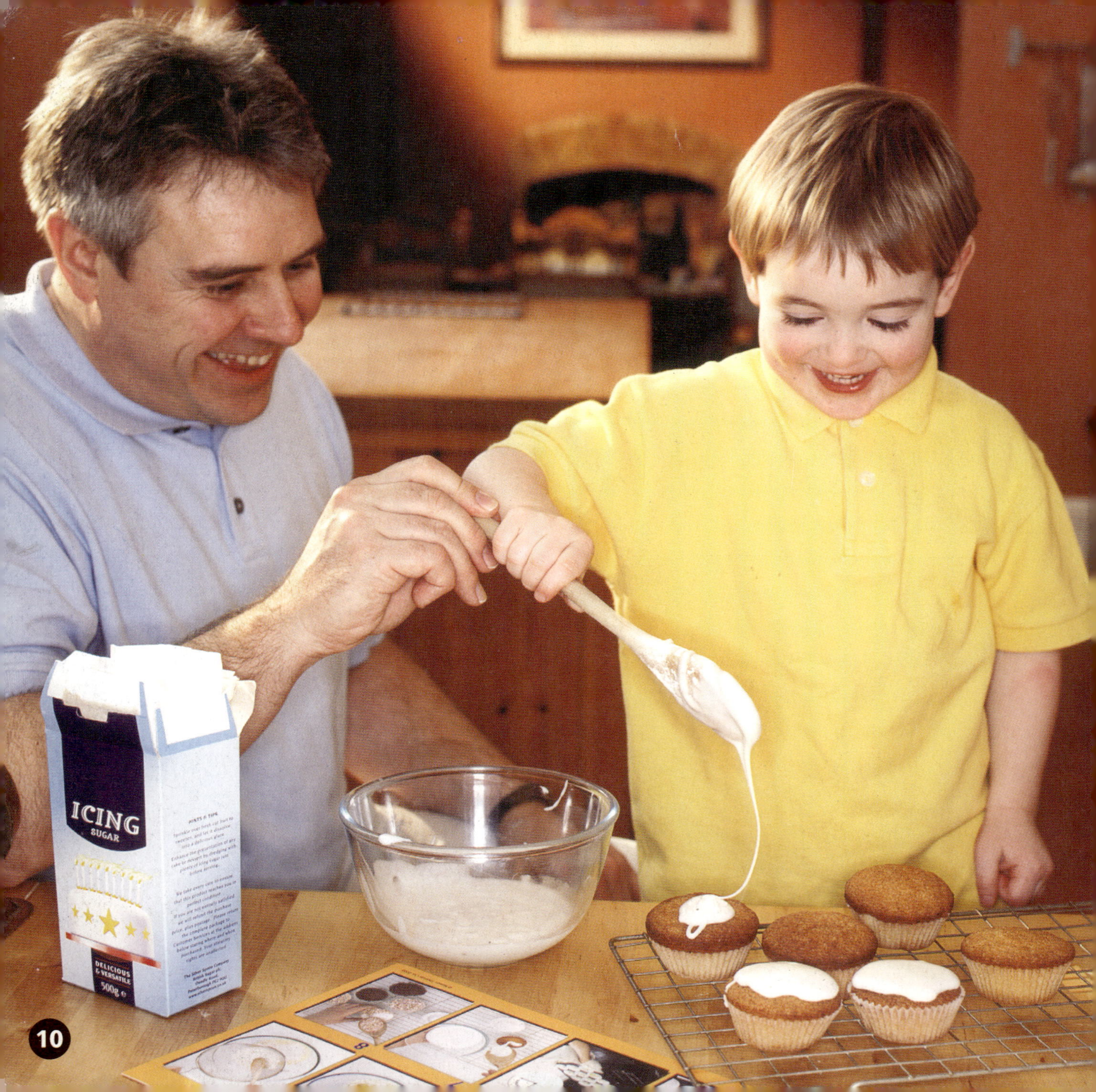
ICING
SUGAR
DELICIOUS & VERSATILE
500g

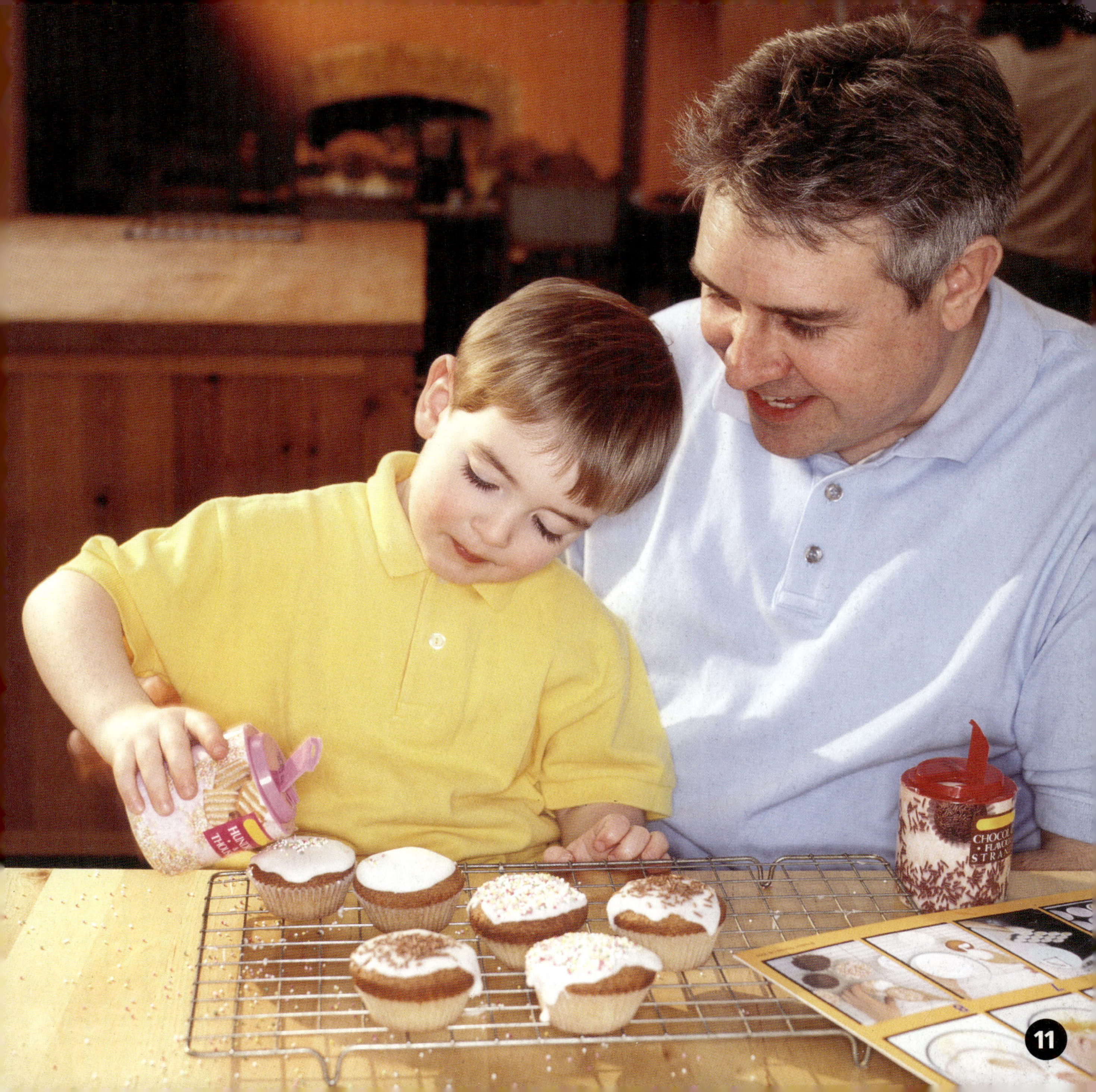

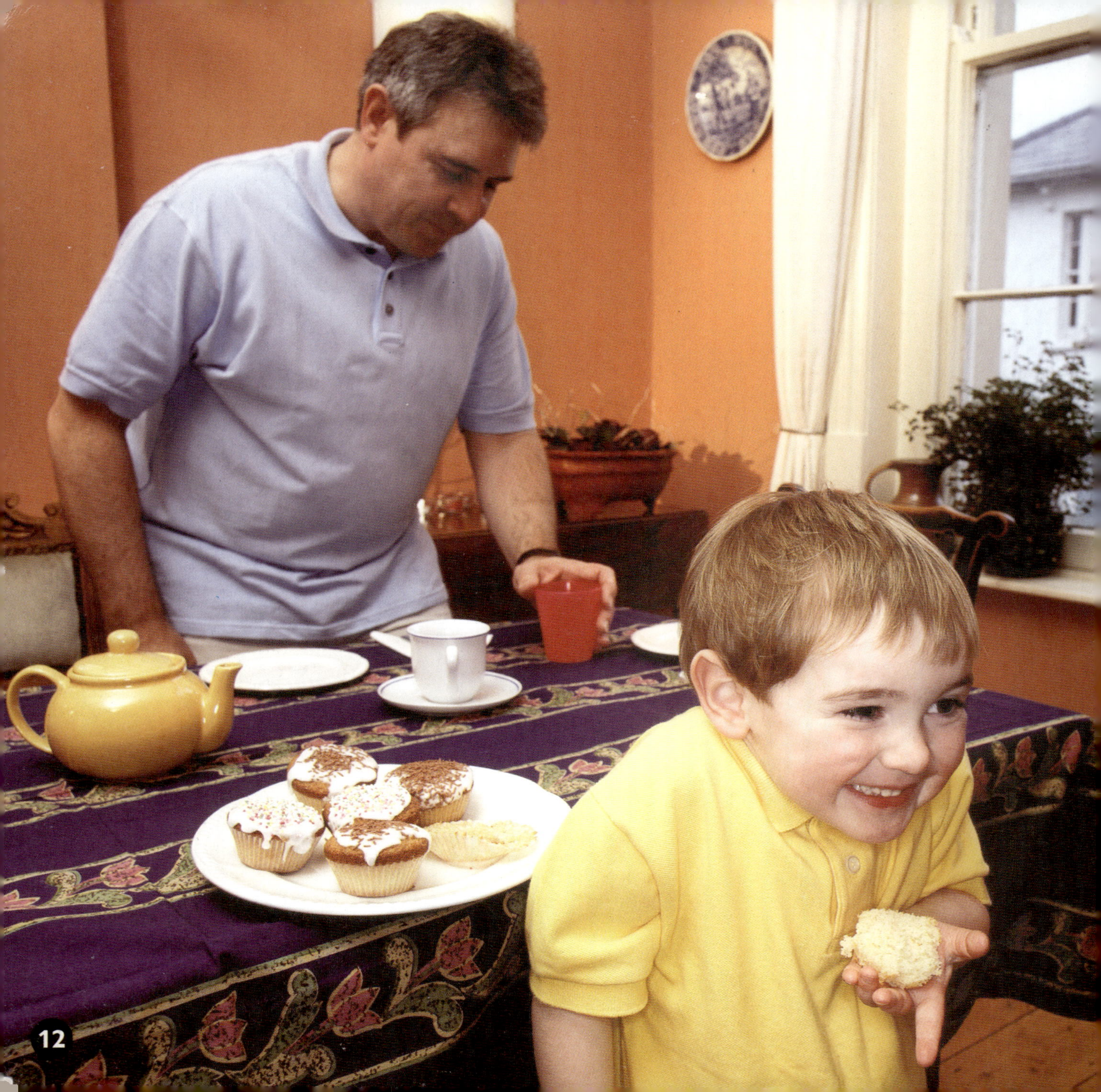